W9-DAN-592

American Indian Children of the Past

AMERICAN INDIAN CHILDREN OF THE PAST

VICTORIA SHERROW

THE MILLBROOK PRESS
BROOKFIELD • CONNECTICUT

Cover photograph courtesy of The Bettmann Archive.

Photographs courtesy of John G. Neihardt Papers, c. 1858–1974, Western Historical Manuscript Collection-Columbia: p. 8; Department of Library Services, American Museum of Natural History, neg. no. 316346, (Rodman Wannamaker): p. 16; Milwaukee Public Museum: p. 19; National Anthropological Archives, Smithsonian Institution: pp. 23 (neg. 487-C), 25 (neg. 1102-B-26), 32 (neg. 1044-A), 38 (neg. 1824-C), 42 (neg. 2433), 47 (neg. 32357-D), 52 (neg. 1668), 56 (neg. 1775-A), 67 (neg. 47749-H), North Wind Picture Archives: p. 27; The Southwest Museum, Los Angeles: p. 37 (N.41687); Museum of Northern Arizona Photo Archives: p. 40 (neg. E111A.75/76.2369, cat. 3159/E7504); The New York Public Library, Special Collections: p. 44 (KF+ + +1907); The Bettmann Archive: p. 54; South Dakota State Historical Society-State Archives: p. 61 (top); Montana Historical Society: p. 61 (bottom); Horner Museum, Oregon State University: p. 68 (no. 6580); Canadian Museum of Civilization: p. 77 (no. 255); FPG International Corporation: p. 81.

Library of Congress Cataloging-in-Publication Data
Sherrow, Victoria.
American Indian children of the past / Victoria Sherrow.
p. cm.
Includes bibliographical references and index.
Summary: Describes what life was like for Indian children growing up in various regions—Northeast Woodlands, Southeast, Southwest, Plains, and Northwest Coast—during the eighteenth, nineteenth, and early twentieth centuries.
ISBN 0-7613-0033-3 (lib. bdg.)
1. Indian children—North America—History—Juvenile literature.
2. Indian children—North America—Social life and customs—Juvenile literature. [1. Indians of North America.] I. Title.
E98.C5S54 1997
973'.0497'0083—dc20 96-34619 CIP AC

Published by The Millbrook Press
2 Old New Milford Road, Brookfield, Connecticut 06804

5 4 3 2 1

Contents

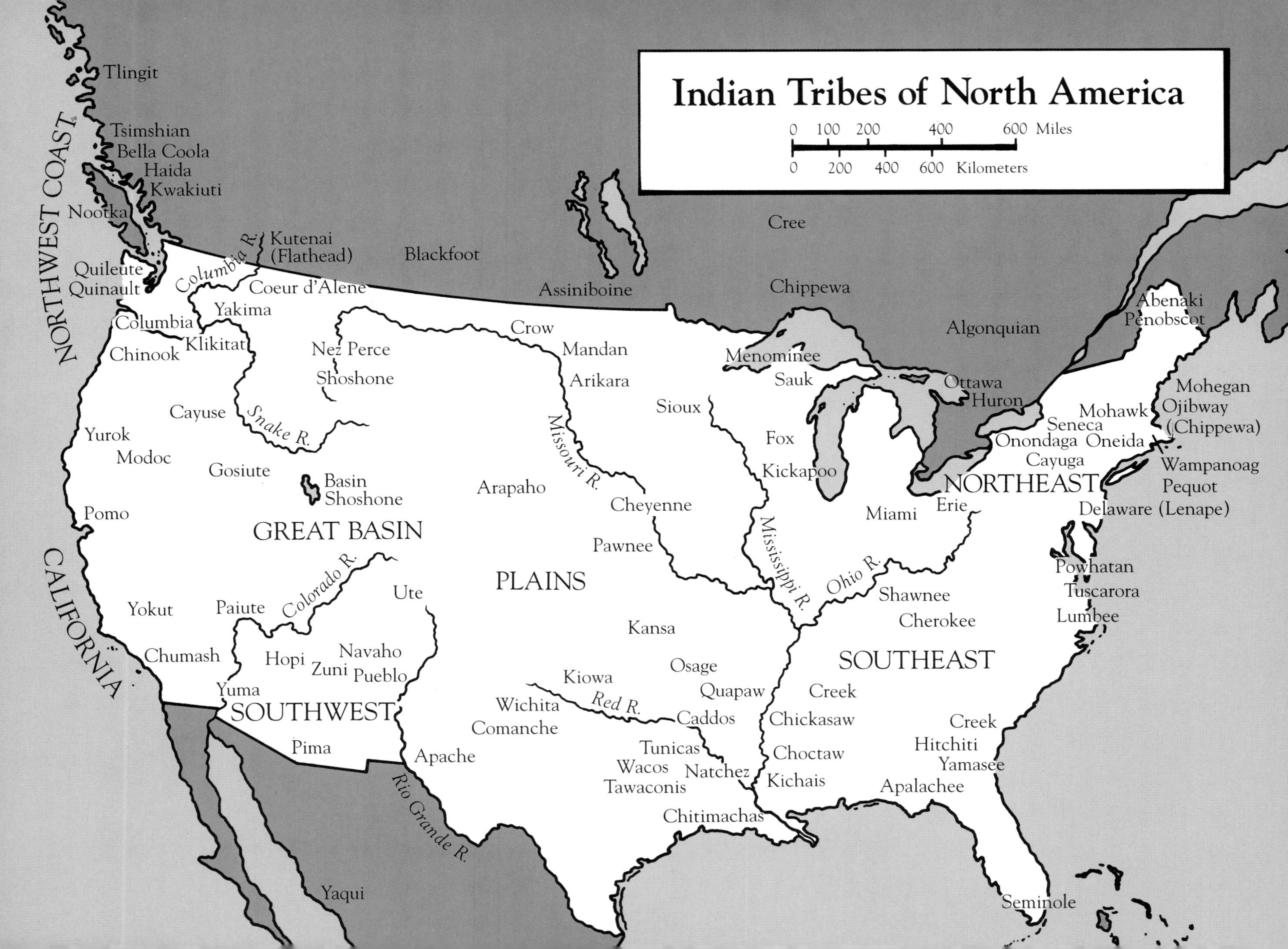

Indian Tribes of North America
0 100 200 400 600 Miles
0 200 400 600 Kilometers
NORTHWEST COAST
Tlingit
Tsimshian
Bella Coola
Haida
Kwakiuti
Nootka
Quileute
Quinault
Columbia
Chinook
Columbia R.
Kutenai (Flathead)
Blackfoot
Coeur d'Alene
Yakima
Klikitat
Nez Perce
Shoshone
Cayuse
Snake R.
Yurok
Modoc
Gosiute
Basin Shoshone
Pomo
GREAT BASIN
CALIFORNIA
Colorado R.
Yokut
Paiute
Ute
Chumash
Hopi
Navaho
Zuni
Pueblo
Yuma
SOUTHWEST
Pima
Yaqui
Rio Grande R.
Apache
Assiniboine
Crow
Mandan
Arikara
Missouri R.
Arapaho
Cheyenne
Pawnee
PLAINS
Kansa
Kiowa
Red R.
Wichita
Comanche
Osage
Quapaw
Caddos
Tunicas
Wacos
Tawaconis
Natchez
Chitimachas
Cree
Chippewa
Sioux
Menominee
Sauk
Fox
Kickapoo
Mississippi R.
Miami
Erie
Ohio R.
Algonquian
Ottawa
Huron
Abenaki
Penobscot
Mohegan
Ojibway (Chippewa)
Mohawk
Seneca
Onondaga
Oneida
Cayuga
NORTHEAST
Wampanoag
Pequot
Delaware (Lenape)
Powhatan
Tuscarora
Lumbee
Shawnee
Cherokee
SOUTHEAST
Creek
Chickasaw
Choctaw
Kichais
Creek
Hitchiti
Yamasee
Apalachee
Seminole

Introduction

Whether helping to plant rows of corn in the Northeast, riding a spotted pony on the Plains, or gathering clams in the Pacific Northwest, Native American children experienced a unique way of life in their traditional cultures. Growing up, they knew both freedom and security, as well as plenty of challenges and hard work.

Before white settlers covered the continent of North America, there were more than 300 different tribal groups. These tribes are divided into what are called culture areas, based on where and how they lived. North American culture groups include the Northeast Woodlands, the Southeast, the Southwest, the Great Plains, the Far West, and the Northwest Coast. The regions these groups lived in had different climates and natural resources. The people raised, gathered, and hunted different kinds of food.

All Native Americans shared certain beliefs yet had their own distinct customs and lifestyles. In common, they viewed life as a circle, without beginning or end, that connected all things in an endless hoop. The circle embraced humans, animals, and plants, all depending on one another.

As they grew up, Native American children learned about this circle of life and their place in it. Revealing the life-view that he learned as a child, the Oglala Sioux holy man Black Elk called his life "the story . . . of us two-leggeds

Black Elk, the famous Oglala Sioux holy man. At age nine, Black Elk saw a vision that inspired him to devote his life to renewing the seven sacred rights of his people.

sharing in it with the four-leggeds and the wings of the air and all green things; for these are children of one mother and their father is one Spirit."[1]

The daily lives of Indian children depended greatly on their surroundings and the ways of nature. What kinds of wild foods could be gathered? Could crops be grown? Was water plentiful or scarce? Was there game or fish to catch and eat? Would they have to prepare for a harsh winter? Santee Sioux George Eastman (also known as Ohiyesa, which means "the winner") described the way he and his friends gained knowledge about their surroundings:

> We were close students of nature. We studied the habits of animals just as you study your books. We watched the men of our people and represented them in our play; then learned to emulate them in our lives.[2]

Time was measured not with clocks but in terms of the seasons and the movements of the sun and moon. As Black Elk said, "I was born in the Moon of the Popping Trees," the month we call December.[3] Unusual events marked unnumbered years in the past, as when Pacific coastal tribes spoke of "The Winter of the Hundred Slain," referring to a battle in which 100 men were killed.

The family was at the center of Native American life. Babies were eagerly welcomed and whole villages often celebrated a birth. Plains Indians said that children were more valuable than horses, weapons, or fine tepees. Grandparents often played an important role from the first moments of a child's life. Hopi grandmothers marked the four walls of the room with cornmeal after a child was born. Plains grandmothers gave a newborn its first bath, rubbing its skin with buffalo grease.

Children were seldom lonely. Besides their parents and siblings, they were closely involved with their extended families, clans, and villages. The entire community took an active part in raising children.

Children were encouraged to become independent. They could usually roam their villages or explore the woods, hills, or plains after chores were done. When they were able, they learned to swim, ride a horse, paddle a canoe, and perform other tasks that were useful to their tribe. Adults would lend a hand, offer advice, or give a scolding if a child misbehaved.

In most tribes, children were asked to do things, rather than being given orders. Knowing clearly what was expected of them, Indian children were generally well behaved. Of course, in a close-knit community, it was difficult to hide misdeeds. Instead of physical punishment, people in the community usually shamed or embarrassed the wrong-doer with teasing and ridicule. By the same token, good deeds were praised and rewarded.

As they grew up, young people had well-defined tasks and roles at each stage of their lives. Special ceremonies, varying from tribe to tribe, marked the passage from childhood to adulthood.

Spirituality was an integral part of these ceremonies, as with all aspects of daily life. For example, Iroquois laws explained to young people how to maintain a proper relationship with their Creator and other supernatural beings. Some ceremonies were held to ask the spirits for help, while others aimed to ward off evil. At ceremonies throughout the year, people gave thanks for the gifts of nature. Observing these ceremonies, young children were awed by the elaborate costumes, music, and rituals. As they grew older, they took a more active part.

Perhaps the greatest lesson a child learned was to place the well-being of the community above individual wants and needs. Among the Tlingit of the Northwest Coast, for instance, it was an honor to hunt for food to share with the elderly or with women whose husbands had died. A young Plains Indian who killed a buffalo for those in need earned the approval of his village. Besides learning to be unselfish, children were told to follow certain rules in order to grow up wisely and well: Treat your elders with respect. Be honest. Do not lose your temper. Be kind to others. Speak softly. Be brave.

Children learned about such virtues and about their history and traditions as they watched their elders and heard tribal songs, stories, myths, and legends that passed from one generation to the next. In these ways, they learned the ancient customs of their people. And always, their elders would say, "Someday, you will teach these things to your own children . . ."

Chapter One

Growing Up in the Northeast Woodlands

On a hot summer day in 1760, in what is now western New York State, several Seneca children followed their elders to the cornfields. Bean vines curled up around the cornstalks, while squash plants, with their twisting stems and broad green leaves, grew closer to the ground.

In the spring, the women and young girls of the village had planted corn, bean, and squash seeds. These plants were known as the Three Sisters or Our Supporters. The children were often told how these foods had sustained their ancestors for centuries.

But lately, rain had been scarce, and the Seneca were worried. They had gathered at the fields to pray to Grandfather He'-no, the Thunder God. Young girls and their mothers poured water around the cornstalks while an older, respected woman led the prayer:

> Oh, He'-no, our Grandfather,
> Come to us and speak kindly,
> Come to us and wash the earth again.

When the soil is too dry
The corn cannot grow.
The beans and squashes are dry and withered
Because they are thirsty.
For all thy gifts,
We thank thee.

Come to thy grandchildren—
Bring rain, bring rain!

With luck, rain would fall, and the people would give thanks. Their harvest would yield enough food for young and old alike.

The Senecas were the largest tribe in the powerful Iroquois Confederacy, which also included the Mohawk, Onondaga, Oneida, and Cayuga. The Tuscaroras joined the confederacy in 1712. Among the other tribes in the Iroquoian language and culture group were the Erie and Huron. In addition to the Iroquois, there was another major group called the Algonquian. This group included such tribes as the Ojibway (or Chippewa), Abenaki (including the Penobscot), Wampanoag, Pequot, Mohegan, Ottawa, Cree, Kickapoo, Menominee, Fox, Miami, Sauk, Shawnee, Delaware (or Lenape), and Powhatan. Known as the Northeast Woodland culture group, they lived in present-day New England, the central Atlantic states, and the Great Lakes area.

Homes and Villages

The Northeast was a land of dense forests, filled with birch, maple, oak, and beech, as well as pines, spruces, and other evergreens. From these woods came materials for homes. Wigwams were made from saplings bent into a rounded frame and tied with pieces of leather, then covered with bark. Longhouses, popular among the Iroquois, were made of wood planks and covered with bark, often from elm trees.

Children lived with their parents and maternal (meaning on their mother's side) grandparents. Families shared rooms along the sides of the longhouses, while central areas provided meeting places for leaders or larger groups.

Towns, made up of several wigwams or longhouses, were located near a source of water. Iroquois villages were surrounded by log walls and moats to keep out enemies. Tribes that farmed had a reliable source of food and could build permanent homes.

Spirituality and Legends

From an early age, children knew their clan membership, which came from their mother. Over the doorway of an Iroquois longhouse was the group's clan symbol, often a Turtle, Bear, or Wolf. Other clans in the Northeast included the Beaver, Deer, Eel, Heron, and Hawk.

Old tales featured these animals and other spiritual beings. A turtle played a key role in Iroquois and Ojibway creation stories.

One such story said that after a great flood had covered the world, Sky Woman came to earth to help the animals. She landed on a turtle and asked Muskrat to gather earth, which she spread on the turtle's back. It grew into a large island, which became the Earth, and Sky Woman gave birth to the first humans.

Iroquois storytellers enthralled audiences of children with tales of Naked Bear, Monster Mosquito, the Great Horned Serpent, and other supernatural creatures. Many stories showed the forces of good fighting forces of evil. A major part of a child's education, these stories also taught them to be skillful storytellers themselves.

These Indians had no written language but used picture-writing and symbols. Iroquois children could examine strings of shells and beads that had been cut and polished, then arranged on belts in meaningful designs. Tribal elders used them to teach children about laws and history. One belt from the 1700s shows five white circles, one for each Iroquois nation, on a background of purple beads.

Childhood

Babies were strapped to wooden cradleboards, which mothers carried with them during the day. Propped against tree trunks, they could watch the activities around them. From time to time, their mothers stopped to nurse them. Hung on Ojibway cradleboards were sacred objects, such as tiny drums or bows and arrows, that had been given to the babies by their namers—members of the tribe who chose protective names for newborns.

As she goes about her daily activities, an Ojibway (Chippewa) woman can take along her baby, safely strapped on this beautifully decorated cradleboard.

Aside from eating utensils, clothing, and simple toys, children owned few material things. They might have some tools or a basket of their own for carrying things. They had a few pieces of deerskin clothing, sometimes dyed red or blue and decorated with porcupine quills. Jewelry was made from copper and seashells. Girls rubbed bear oil onto their long hair to make it gleam.

Whatever the season, older children had numerous chores. They gathered firewood for cooking and warmth. With wooden buckets, they brought fresh water from the springs to use for cooking, drinking, and washing.

Fall was an especially busy time, getting ready for the cold winter ahead. Children helped with hunting and harvesting, drying and smoking meat, and stretching and scraping animal skins. They filled baskets with acorns, hickory nuts, beechnuts, and chestnuts. Nuts were ground into flour to store for winter meals. Children also gathered milkweed and other fibrous plants that were made into twine.

A hearty supper of succotash, a dish made with beans and corn, might end the day. The Seneca liked to say that a meal would "lie well on the tongue" after a hard day's work. Children or adults who failed to do their share might not receive their evening meal.

Raising Food

Northeast Indians used their knowledge of nature to plan their lives, especially when it came to raising crops. The Seneca planted corn when the first oak leaves were the size of a red squirrel's foot. Algonquians liked to begin planting when oak leaves were about the size of a mouse's ear.

Iroquois girls and women sowed crops carefully for a good harvest. They poked holes in the soil with their digging sticks and placed seeds inside. Rows of corn were set in small hills about three feet apart, and bean and squash seeds were later planted in the same hills. The vines entwined themselves around the rising cornstalks, making it easier to pull weeds and harvest crops. Children also caught hundreds of small fish to place in the soil as fertilizer.

As the crops grew, children spent hours weeding and tending them. Mary Jemison, a white child from Pennsylvania who was captured by Seneca Indians in 1758 and chose to stay with them, later described her experiences. In *Indian Captive: The Story of Mary Jemison,* Lois Lenski recounts the instructions Mary and other children were given about their work in the fields: "First, there are the weeds, rank and tall, who try to choke its roots. They must be pulled out and destroyed. After three weedings the corn is safe. Now that the ears are beginning to form, there are thieves who come to steal—birds, squirrels, field mice, crows, deer."[1]

Children took turns scaring away crows and other animals by shouting and waving a blanket in the air. They saw the seeds grow to ripe vegetables. They also went into the woods to look for wild foods like berries, fruits, and roots.

Late summer was a busy time for corn-growing village bands. Children helped to pick and husk the corn and then set it to dry outdoors on wooden planks. The whole community came together for their most sacred holiday, the Green Corn Festival, which lasted several days. The festival began with a fast, after which the Iroquois enjoyed a special feast featuring fresh, sweet corn, along with songs and games. Babies who had been born since midwinter received their names during the festival.

For the Ojibway and other Great Lakes tribes, wild rice was a staple food. Rice grew in swamps, ponds, and shallow lakes in the Northeast, and people harvested it from their canoes in late summer. Children then helped to spread the rice out to dry. Next, the rice was put in a big kettle and parched over a fire to loosen the grain from the husks.

MAPLE SUGARING TIME

In early spring, children looked forward to making maple sugar. Each family tapped the group of trees their ancestors had used. Based on Mary Jemison's account of life among the Seneca, Lois Lenski writes,

> With crooked sticks, broad and sharp at the end, the women stripped bark from a felled elm tree and made many new boat-shaped vessels, each holding about two gallons. The men notched the maple trees with their tomahawks, driving in long hardwood chips to carry the sap away from the trees. The children ran back and forth setting the bark vessels at the bases of the tree trunks to catch the flowing sap. . . . Each day's run had to be carried to the camp.[2]

At the sugar camp, sap was poured into pots set over open fires. Young people stirred the fragrant sap as it simmered, thickening into syrup, and then turning into sugar which was then set in molds and stored as small cakes. The cakes were used to flavor cornmeal and other foods. Children could not resist dropping some hot syrup on the snow, where it hardened into tasty candy.

A ceremony of thanksgiving for the maple harvest was held once they returned to the village. People gathered around a great campfire in front of the longhouses as the chief spoke:

> We thank thee, Great Spirit,
> For sending the soft winds and fair breezes
> To melt the snow and make sweet waters flow
> From the heart of the Maple.

Children in the Northeast, Southeast, and parts of the northern Plains helped to collect maple sap and make it into maple sugar. This natural sweetener added variety to their diets.

Hunting for Game

While girls helped to raise crops, boys in the Northeast learned to hunt and fish and to make canoes and weapons. Young men looked forward to providing game for the tribe. Penobscot boys began hunting at about age six. A boy who killed his first rabbit was honored at a party where others ate some rabbit, but he did not. It was thought that if he did, he would not be lucky enough to catch another one.

A successful autumn hunt caused great rejoicing. Children ran out to meet the hunting party. Had they brought deer, rabbits, moose, maybe a bear? Some meat was eaten fresh, while other pieces were dried and stored for winter, a time when game might be scarce.

An important midwinter ceremony was held after the hunt to start a new year. This four-day ceremony began as people called faith keepers visited each longhouse to announce the start and bid people to clean their homes. People then visited their neighbors carrying paddles, used to stir the ashes in their fire pits. The faith keepers also stirred the ashes in every home and offered thanks to the Creator for keeping people safe that year.

Surviving the Winter

In preparation for winter, corn was stored underground, below the frost line, in holes lined with layers of birch bark. Slices of squash and pumpkin, and certain berries, meat, and fish also were dried and stored underground.

Cornmeal was eaten often during the winter. Like other tribes, the Seneca sometimes boiled corncakes in water. The cooking water was then served as a soup along with the cakes. At mealtimes, children used wooden bowls and ladles, some with decorative carving on the end.

Winter was a time for special ceremonies, storytelling, and games that could be played in cold weather or in the snow. Cold winter evenings were also a good time to make twine, clothing, baskets, and other tools, weapons, or household items.

To find game during the winter, the Penobscot of present-day Maine moved from their summer villages to areas deep in the woods. Children helped to load the birchbark canoes so the family could leave before ice made the rivers unpassable. When they arrived, fires were started from pieces of smoldering wood that had been brought in closed seashells. Then families set up tepee-shaped wigwams of birch bark.

Moving with the Seasons

When winter ended, Indians who had moved to winter campsites returned to their villages. During the spring, Penobscot bands fished at river falls and rapids for smelt, salmon, and shad. Come summer, they moved to homes along the rocky seacoast. Families camped on the beach, where children enjoyed swimming and playing on the shore.

Throughout the summer, children helped to collect lobsters, clams, and crabs, abundant in their region. These shellfish were cooked over fires on the sand. After a meal, the children helped to throw the empty shells back into the water. The Penobscot and some other tribes believed that shells would become fish once again if they were returned to the sea. As the shells disappeared from sight, the children were told that this was the way of the circle of life.

Games and Recreation

Like children anywhere, Native Americans enjoyed having fun. Playthings were made of wood, cornhusks, and other natural materials. Birch bark was shaped into miniature canoes and containers for toys and small keepsakes. Girls "played house" with small wooden bowls and dolls made from cornhusks or buckskin.

The outdoors provided space for games. Children rolled hoops made of birch bark along the ground. Some games used balls made from animal skins and stuffed with feathers or fur. Iroquois men and boys played stickball, or baggataway, which developed into the modern game of lacrosse. Sticks with webbed ends were used to hurl a hard deerskin ball down a field and across the other team's goal. It was a rough game, with goalposts sometimes miles apart!

A popular winter game was snowsnake. Players skimmed a long rod carved from hardwood (the snake) along areas of smooth snow or a frozen lake. Sometimes darts or spears were used instead of wooden rods. The winner was the player whose "snake" glided the farthest.

Coming of Age

At the time of puberty, a young man sought to have a vision during a ritual called a vision quest. He spent about four days in the forest, fasting with only small amounts of water. He hoped the dreams that came in the night would reveal a guardian spirit to guide and protect him during his life. Guardian spirits could give their owners power in times of danger, sickness, or need.

At puberty, a young woman spent several days alone in a small wigwam that her mother built away from the main village. In the hut, she communicated with the spirit world, asking to be blessed with a long life, a good husband, and many children. During this time, the girl ate almost no food but drank some water.

Ojibway birchbark canoes. The thick bark needed for these canoes was taken from large trees, while thinner birchbark was made into containers and other items.

As they approached adulthood, young men refined their hunting and fishing skills. Teenage boys began building a canoe. Canoes were used for recreation as well as for fishing and travel. Some were carved out of tree trunks, while others were fashioned of birch bark. Sheets of bark from white birch trees were laid on the ground and folded around the wooden frame. A young man might spend many hours building a craft that would last for years. Paddles were carved from ash, beech, and maple wood.

By adolescence, young people of the eastern woodlands had gained the knowledge and skills needed for adulthood. They were ready to assume their roles as husbands and wives, raise families of their own, and pass on the traditions and beliefs that guided the lives of individuals, families, and their community.

Chapter Two

Growing Up in the Southeast

During the year 1750, in what is now eastern Tennessee, a young Cherokee boy and his grandfather walked toward the river. At age six, the boy was old enough to make his first hunting weapon, a blowgun. At the river, he looked for a piece of hollow river cane. With the older man's help, the boy smoothed out the inside of the cane. Back at the village, he learned how to make darts from pieces of hardwood that fit inside the blowgun tube.

In time, he was ready to try hunting. Aiming his blowgun at squirrels or rabbits, he blew strong puffs of air through the tube to send the dart toward his prey. With practice, the boy learned to use this tool to bring food home, gaining approval from his family.

The Cherokee were one of the largest groups in the Muskogean family, which also included the Chickasaw, Seminole, Choctaw, Alabama, Creek, Natchez, Hitchiti, Yamasee, Apalachee, Houmas, Tunica, and Chitimacha.

Joe Silestine (Toshkachito), a Choctaw living in Louisiana, uses a long blowgun made of cane. Darts sent through this blowgun could travel a distance of twenty-five feet.

Other groups were the Lumbee, Caddo, Kichai, Waco, and Quapaw. They lived in present-day West Virginia, Virginia, Maryland, Tennessee, North and South Carolina, Georgia, Alabama, Mississippi, Arkansas, Louisiana, Texas, and Florida.

Homes and Villages

Children of the southeastern tribes enjoyed a mild climate and a land rich in plants and animals—squirrels, bears, deer, birds, and fish. The fertile soil made for abundant crops, and the tribes that lived here prospered. A steady food supply enabled people to build permanent villages.

Homes were rectangular in shape and made of thatch. Cherokee villages might stretch for miles along a river. A council house located in the center of the village was used for ceremonies, celebrations, political meetings, and other community gatherings.

Children lived in extended families in the homes of their mothers and their mother's relatives. Belonging to the mother's clan gave a Cherokee child membership in the tribe.

Spirituality and Legends

As in other Indian groups, religious ceremonies were an ongoing part of life. Southeastern children learned about their religious traditions and tribal history through stories.

Cherokee children learned that the world had been created when a large island of mud formed on the back of a water beetle. A buzzard flew down from the sky, where all beings had once lived, and flapped his wings upon the mud, creating valleys and mountains. Plants and animals from the sky came down to live on the newly formed Earth, as did the first man and woman, Kana'ti and Selu.

Such stories explained how the world worked and how people should relate to each other and to their surroundings. Religious ceremonies gave people a sense of peace and security. They provided chances to give thanks for blessings, as the Creek, Seminole, and Cherokee did at the annual Green Corn Festival, and to ask spirits for help. By observing and taking part, children learned what was expected of them as they grew up.

Childhood

As in other regions, Cherokee babies were strapped on cradleboards and carried about during the day. Cradleboards served another purpose among the Choctaw, Chickasaw, Caddo, and Catawba. Males in these groups had flattened foreheads. This shape was achieved by binding the baby's head against the cradleboard so that it pressed against the developing skullbones.

AH-YOKA AND THE CHEROKEE ALPHABET

In 1809, a Cherokee scholar named Sequoyah set out to develop a written language for his people. Sequoyah had become intrigued by what he called the "talking leaves of the white man"—pieces of paper covered with ink markings. He thought the Cherokee, too, should have a way to preserve stories on paper and to communicate across long distances.

At first, Sequoyah spent weeks drawing pictures on bark of various words used by the Cherokee. But this was time-consuming and seemed an inefficient way to send messages. One day, his daughter Ah-Yoka showed him an old English spelling book she had found in the woods. While studying this book, Sequoyah realized that the twenty-six characters he saw throughout the book were used to form words. He devised a group of eighty-five symbols to represent syllables in the Cherokee language.

By 1821, after years of effort, Sequoyah was ready to share his sound alphabet with his tribe. Before it could be used, he needed the approval of the Cherokee Tribal Council. With Ah-Yoka's help, he showed them how the system worked. She accompanied him to a special meeting. While she was out of the room, Cherokee chiefs directed her father to write down messages, using his symbols.

Ah-Yoka returned to the room and amazed the council members by correctly reading the words that the chiefs had dictated. The council immediately approved the alphabet. Thanks to Sequoyah and Ah-Yoka, Cherokee children and adults could learn to read and write in their own language.

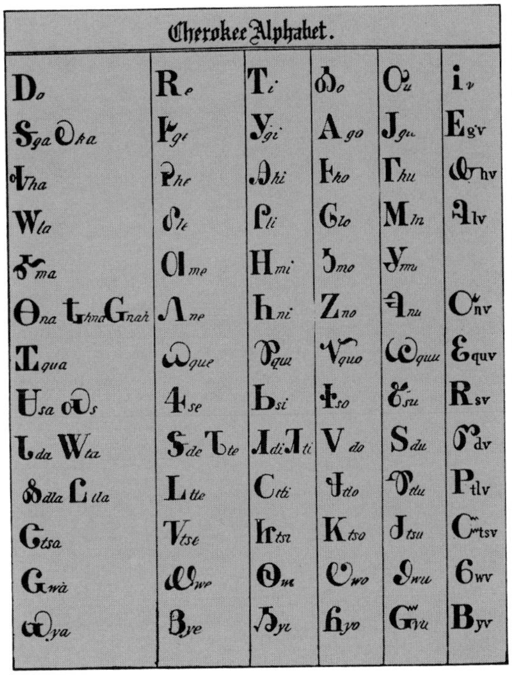

Cherokee Alphabet.

Ꭰ a	Ꭱ e	Ꭲ i	Ꭳ o	Ꭴ u	Ꭵ v
Ꭶ ga Ꭷ ka	Ꭸ ge	Ꭹ gi	Ꭺ go	Ꭻ gu	Ꭼ gv
Ꭽ ha	Ꭾ he	Ꭿ hi	Ꮀ ho	Ꮁ hu	Ꮂ hv
Ꮃ la	Ꮄ le	Ꮅ li	Ꮆ lo	Ꮇ lu	Ꮈ lv
Ꮉ ma	Ꮊ me	Ꮋ mi	Ꮌ mo	Ꮍ mu	
Ꮎ na Ꮏ hna Ꮐ nah	Ꮑ ne	Ꮒ ni	Ꮓ no	Ꮔ nu	Ꮕ nv
Ꮖ qua	Ꮗ que	Ꮘ qui	Ꮙ quo	Ꮚ quu	Ꮛ quv
Ꮜ sa Ꮝ s	Ꮞ se	Ꮟ si	Ꮠ so	Ꮡ su	Ꮢ sv
Ꮣ da Ꮤ ta	Ꮥ de Ꮦ te	Ꮧ di Ꮨ ti	Ꮩ do	Ꮪ du	Ꮫ dv
Ꮬ dla Ꮭ tla	Ꮮ tle	Ꮯ tli	Ꮰ tlo	Ꮱ tlu	Ꮲ tlv
Ꮳ tsa	Ꮴ tse	Ꮵ tsi	Ꮶ tso	Ꮷ tsu	Ꮸ tsv
Ꮹ wa	Ꮺ we	Ꮻ wi	Ꮼ wo	Ꮽ wu	Ꮾ wv
Ꮿ ya	Ᏸ ye	Ᏹ yi	Ᏺ yo	Ᏻ yu	Ᏼ yv

Sequoyah spent ten years developing the Cherokee alphabet, with its eighty-five symbols.

After babies received the spirit name of an ancestor, a string of small white beads was placed around their necks to signify this event. Yuchi newborns were watched closely during the first week of life, days when they were thought to be closely linked to the spirit world. Twins were watched for signs that they had special supernatural powers. A twin who showed signs of such powers was prepared for life as a healer or spiritual leader.

Child-rearing duties were shared by all the mothers. Older girls helped to tend the younger children. Mothers usually nursed children until they were about two years old.

In warm weather, children younger than four did not wear clothing. At about age four or five, boys began to wear a breechclout, a length of animal skin wrapped around the hips. At this age, boys and girls were separated so that they could learn their special roles and duties as members of their tribes.

Growing boys were taught by men in their mother's clan, especially her brothers (the boys' uncles). The goal was to give all boys similar training and education and impart the virtues of honor, courage, and loyalty to the tribe.

Growing girls were taught by women in the tribe. Creek girls learned from the oldest aunt on their mother's side of the family. Girls also looked to their mother's mother for wisdom and guidance, especially among the Seminole. Young women were urged to develop a pleasant disposition, mild temper, industriousness, and modesty.

Children were not treated harshly or spanked. Adults might scratch a naughty child with a thorn, but the Cherokee thought striking or screaming at children was disrespectful. John Ehle describes the respect shown to Cherokee boys, saying,

> Even as a baby and as a naked young boy playing in the town streets he was honored, highly regarded, a hus-

> band-to-be, a lord someday of a village, a powerful person just now little who would have authority over his own being and the life and death of others.[1]

It was believed that shaming, teasing, or cajoling promoted good behavior. James Adair, a Scotch-Irish trader who observed family life among southeastern tribes during the 1730s, also noted that adults used "sweet" words, saying them "so good-naturedly and skilfully, that they [the children] would sooner die by torture than renew their shame by repeating the actions."[2]

Boys began early to learn their future roles as hunters, fishermen, builders, craftsmen, and warriors. Males provided these services first to their families, then to the community, as needed. They cut trees, cleared and tilled fields, and erected homes and community buildings. They made moccasins, canoes, farming tools, blowguns, bows and arrows, drums, and pipes. They also learned their roles in the religious ceremonies and activities of the tribe.

Girls, too, learned to make useful objects. By age five, they were usually ready to make mats for the floors of their homes, using pieces of split river cane.

Women of the Southeast were known for their ornate, beautiful clay pottery and woven baskets. Their craftsmanship also showed in their clothing, blankets, and decorated moccasins. Step-by-step, they shared these skills with their daughters.

Six-year-old girls began making clay pots. They learned how to find the right kind of clay from the riverbanks, then patiently mold and shape it. A flattened piece formed the bottom of the pot, then long ropes of clay were coiled around the base from bottom to top.

The pot was given its final shape and smoothed with a wet shell. Tribal designs were often drawn on with a sharp bone or stamped with a carved wooden paddle. Finally, the pot was dried in the sun for at least a day, then placed beside a hot fire to harden. Finishing her first clay pot was a big step for a girl and won much praise from her elders.

By ages nine and ten, girls were weaving baskets of different sizes and designs for storing corn and other foods and for carrying firewood. Making a strong and attractive basket took time and skill. First, river cane or bark from an oak or ash tree was gathered and cut. The log of a young tree provided splints for the basket. Plants or roots were boiled to make vivid colors, used to dye the splints brilliant shades of dark and golden brown, red, or orange. Over the years, girls would refine their weaving skills, becoming faster and more adept.

Like Indian children everywhere, those in the Southeast learned that idleness was wrong. Young Choctaw children heard about tiny supernatural beings who carried off lazy children. The message was clear: Move swiftly! Do not neglect your chores!

Providing Food

As in other regions, children helped to raise and gather food. Tribes living in mountainous and wooded areas ate mostly game and wild plants. Boys helped their fathers with the hunting, while girls filled baskets with nuts, berries, crab apples, wild grapes, acorns, sweet potatoes, and wild rice.

As in the Northeast, there was an annual maple syrup harvest. Another natural sweetener, honey, was gathered with care from beehives found in the woods.

Tribes that lived near water—the Natchez, Seminole, and Calusa, for example—fished for many meals. Boys learned to make nets and hooks and to catch fish that swam in lakes, rivers, and along the Atlantic coast. Children gathered clams, crabs, and other shellfish along the shore.

Among the Cherokee and other farming tribes, women and girls raised vegetables. In some tribes both men and women planted crops. Then, females tended the fields, and people of both genders helped with the harvest. Among the Creek, boys under age fifteen worked alongside their mothers. After Creek men planted corn, melons, and sweet potatoes, women and children tended the fields daily.

As the crops ripened, children worked hard to chase away animals. According to William Bartram, an Englishman who lived among the Seminole during the 1770s, children scared away blackbirds and other intruders by "whooping and halooing" at them.[3]

Corn, the main crop, could be eaten in dozens of ways, either fresh or dried, and it stored well. Women and girls used a mortar and pestle to grind the dried kernels. Mortars were made from hollowed-out tree trunks; the pestles, for pounding, were fashioned from bone, wood, or stone. The ground corn was sifted, and then either stored or used for a meal.

English trader Henry Timberlake spent much time among the Cherokee. His *Memoirs,* published in 1765, described abundant meals that included venison, bear, potatoes, corn, peas, pumpkins, and beans. He said that Cherokee bread had "as great perfection" as that baked in "any European oven."[4] There were also melons, cherries, pears, plums, and peaches.

Among the Seminole, William Bartram ate venison, corn cakes, bear's ribs, fish, turkey, and a tasty jelly made of China briar roots and honey.[5] Clearly, children in the Southeast enjoyed a rich variety of foods.

Games and Recreation

With an abundance of food, southeastern Indians had more time for recreation. Males played rigorous outdoor games,

These Cherokees are taking part in a pre-ballgame dance in 1888. The women's dance leader sits by a drum, while the men's leader is shaking a gourd rattle. The ball sticks that will be used in the game are hanging on the rack.

such as stickball (later lacrosse), which they called "the little brother of war." After playing stickball, boys and men performed a religious ritual known as the Stomp Dance, making slow, shuffling movements around a fire.

Stickball was played each July as part of the Green Corn Festival held to celebrate the harvest. At that time, southeastern Indians danced, played games, and enjoyed a great feast featuring roasted fresh corn. With their families and friends, young people took special baths in the river to prepare for the coming year.

There were other games both for males and females. While visiting a village in Virginia in October 1711, William Byrd II saw Native American boys having an archery contest while girls were running foot races.[6] These were not just a source of recreation but were skills the men needed as hunters and warriors and helped girls grow strong and fit for motherhood. Athletics also helped to prepare people to defend themselves against enemies.

Coming of Age

Several traditions marked the move into adulthood. Creek and Choctaw boys were tattooed. Caddo girls were also tattooed as they reached puberty, with large flower designs made by tribal artists. Some bands pierced young people's ear lobes so that special ornaments could be worn. Catawba girls learned how to wear feathers in special ways, and girls in some groups were allowed to grow their hair to new, longer lengths. Choctaw young men were taught how to apply ceremonial paint in colors of red, black, and white.

Looking toward adult life, many boys in the Southeast aspired to be brave, honored warriors. They might go into battle for the first time at age fifteen. Those who proved themselves worthy were then allowed to hunt and fish with the men. Successful warriors received fine headdresses of white feathers and might be allowed to wear special face paint or tattoos.

Young girls looked forward to marriage, for which they could choose their own partner, and to raising children. Women in these tribes knew that their contributions would be valued as much as those of their husbands as they took their places as adults in their communities.

Chapter Three

Growing Up in the Southwest

Early in May, sometime in the mid-1600s, children in a Pueblo village saw the Sun Watcher moving about and shouting the news:

> Let the heavens be covered with clouds;
> Let thunder be heard over the earth.

This announcement meant that the danger of frost was past and planting could begin. From watching where the sun rose over the years, the Sun Watcher was able to judge when winter was truly over.

Hearing the news, boys joined their fathers to travel to the fields with digging sticks and fawn-skin bags holding corn seeds. Once there, the group said special prayers. One man placed a prayer stick meant to bring rain in the middle of the field. With enough rain, hard work, and luck, the life-giving crops would grow.

There were two major groups of Pueblo Indians in the Southwest. The western Pueblos included the Hopi, Zuni, and Taos. Among the Rio Grande Pueblos were the Keres, Tewa, Tiwa, and Towa. They built their villages, called *pueblos,* in what is now Arizona and New Mexico.

Other groups living in the Southwest included the Pima and Tohono O'odham (Papago) as well as the Yuma. The Navajo and Apache were at first nomadic (wandering) groups. The Navajo settled down as farmers and sheepherders, while most of the Apache remained nomadic. The Southwest culture area extended from Arizona and New Mexico south into northern Mexico and Texas.

Homes and Villages

Southwestern lands could be hot and dry, with cool or cold nights, and harsh winters with some icy blizzards. Despite these drawbacks, southwestern Indian children enjoyed surroundings of striking beauty and brilliant skies, often called the Land of Enchantment.

The Pueblos lived in square or rectangular houses of stone and adobe, a plasterlike substance made out of mud. In the villages, the houses were built together to form two- and three-story apartment buildings. Outside, in front of the apartments, were the village's domed adobe ovens.

Pueblo children were connected to their families, clans, and villages. Children of the Navajo, western Apache, Hopi, and some other Pueblo groups belonged to their mothers' clans. The clan owned springs and farms. Clans regulated many aspects of life, such as marriage. People could not marry someone from their own clan.

Pueblo men and boys were further tied to their *kivas,* groups that held special religious ceremonies in underground chambers called by the same name, *kivas.* Children also had a special ceremonial parent of the same sex, as well as their mother and father.

There were no rich or poor among the Pueblos. All shared the community resources. Children learned to work for the group, a spirit that could be seen in home building. A town crier would announce that someone needed a home. Friends and relatives brought adobe and other materials. People gathered to help. Building began after four eagle feathers had been offered up in prayer and laid beneath the cornerstones.

Unlike the Pueblos, the Navajo and Apache did not live in large settled communities. The Navajo lived in small isolated groups, while the Apache moved around in search of food and game. Navajo homes, called hogans, were wooden lodges covered with earth. The Apache built cone-shaped dwellings called wickiups from tree limbs covered with leaves or other available materials.

Spirituality and Legends

Southwestern tribes had a rich and complex spiritual life and oral history. Ceremonies, held often during every season, might take weeks of planning and last several days and nights. Elaborate costumes and masks and musical accompaniment added excitement and ritual to the ceremonies.

Many spiritual customs were tied to specific geographical features, such as lakes, rocks, caves, and mountains. For the Taos Indians, the Blue Lake was sacred. They tossed bits of turquoise and white seashells into the springs while asking for blessings.

A Hopi legend said that the first people had come from the center of the earth through a cave found on their land. *Kachinas*—invisible spirits—were said to live in the San Francisco Peaks. For six months of the year (February through July), the kachinas came down from the mountain to visit the pueblos.

A view of the Hopi village (pueblo) of Mishongnovi, taken in 1901. Ladders were used to move from one house to the other.

"THE KACHINAS ARE COMING!"

To a Hopi child, the arrival of the kachinas (actually men from the village) sparked great excitement. Children watched them stomp across the roofs, then climb down ladders to the ground. While holy men danced to the roll of drumbeats, the kachinas walked along paths of sacred cornmeal.

Kachinas wore splendid costumes adorned with feathers and beads and colorful masks. They appeared during the bean festival (Powamu) in February and at annual summer ceremonies. At the last dance of the summer festival, they passed out gifts. Girls received kachina dolls, and boys received brightly painted bows and arrows.

Children who misbehaved might worry that the Ogre Kachinas would visit them. Ogre kachinas *(Nataskas)* wore masks with long wooden snouts and bulging eyes, and carried knives and threatened to carry off disobedient children. Glimpsing these fierce-looking kachinas at a ceremony, young children often cried out in fear.

Of course, when they grew up, children learned who the kachinas really were. Older boys and girls were warned not to reveal the secret to younger ones. Approaching adulthood, young people learned many serious aspects of their religion. Pueblo boys spent hours inside the kivas—special underground rooms used for religious purposes—learning their history and myths from older men.

Kachinas at a Hopi bean-planting ceremony in Walpi Pueblo in First Mesa, Arizona, in 1893. These grim-faced "spirits" were among the ogres that children learned to fear if they were disobedient.

As every Pueblo child knew from an early age, rain was all-important, the very essence of life. Many ceremonies were designed to ask the spirits for rain. The solemn, nine-day Hopi Snake Dance was one such ceremony. With their zigzag shapes, snakes were thought to resemble lightning, which comes with rain. Snakes for the dance, including poisonous types, were gathered and brought to the village. During one night, Hopi priests held the live snakes in their mouths while other men patted the animals to keep them from attacking. After the ceremony was over, runners carried the snakes back to the places where they had been found.

Childhood

Pueblo babies wore diapers made of cedar bark. Strapped on cradleboards, they stayed near their mothers. The Hopi loved music, and mothers sang to their children. One lullaby went like this:

> Go to sleep, little sleepy bird,
> Go to sleep,
> Or someone will take you away,
> So you better go to sleep, little bird.

As children grew, they were taught the ways of their people. Hopi children learned to be kind to all living creatures, never cruel or violent. Zuni children were told to "show a shining face, even when unhappy, and to listen to old people, who do not lie, and who know things."[1] According to Richard Erdoes, who spent much time among the Pueblos,

> Children are taught to respect old people; not to wander into a kiva; not to fight, injure or make fun of others; not to hurt animals. Nobody tells them not to say any "bad words" because these simply do not occur in the Indian language. Boys and girls are rarely punished, seldom yelled at, and almost never beaten. They may, however, be teased or shamed into good behavior.[2]

A Hopi kachina doll, wearing an elaborate costume, shows the artistry that went into the carving and dressing of these cottonwood figures.

Until age six, Hopi children were taught by their mothers. Then, from six to ten, boys were initiated into the kachina cult. While standing on a sand painting, the child was whipped by an adult dressed as a kachina, and his ceremonial parents were named. Both boys and girls were given their own kachina doll, known as a *tithu,* carved from cottonwood root and painted in the image of a kachina. These dolls taught children about their heritage and religion.

Up to about age ten, children did not wear clothing during hot weather. After that age, Pueblo girls and boys wore clothing woven of cotton fibers. Navajo clothing was often made of sheep's wool.

As older girls spent more time with adult women, they learned new skills. They began making pottery, moving from simpler to more intricate designs. Women and girls also helped to build homes.

Navajo girls began herding sheep when they were about five years old or when they seemed ready. Gradually, they were given lambs of their own to tend. Children learned to keep track of the animals as they grazed in the hills. During the spring, when sheep were sheared, Navajo children helped to clean the wool. They combed it with tools that had toothlike edges. Before being spun into fibers, the wool was washed with soap made from the roots of the yucca plant.

Navajo women, known as fine weavers, taught their daughters these skills. They made bright dyes for cloth, baskets, and mats from plants and roots. Pueblo, Pima, and Tohono O'odham (Papago) girls began learning to make baskets and mats very young, and to weave and make clothing.

By age seven, boys of the Southwest were hunting, carrying wood, watching sheep, guarding horses, and, if they were Pueblos, weaving. Boys raised crops and learned to ride horses or burros, if they had such animals. They helped to plant and cultivate crops. According to Hopi Don Talayeswa, idleness was "a disgrace," frowned upon by his people. He writes,

> We followed our fathers to the fields and helped plant and weed. The old men took us for walks and taught us the use of plants. . . . We joined the women in gathering rabbitweed for baskets and went with them to dig clay for pots. We watched the fields to drive out the birds and rodents, picked peaches to dry in the sun.[3]

A Navajo child cards wool while one woman weaves a blanket, another spins wool, and a third weaves on a belt frame. Legend said that Spider Woman taught First Woman how to weave, so spiderwebs were rubbed on the hands of baby girls to make them good weavers.

Providing Food

Much of a Hopi or Pueblo child's time was spent helping to plant and harvest corn, squash, and beans. While walking to the fields each day, boys kicked stones along the way. This was supposed to bring rain, since stones fell down the side of the mesa when it was raining. Boys helped their fathers plant corn in deep holes. They weeded with pointed sticks and scared away hungry crows.

When the corn was harvested, children helped to spread the ears—speckled with colors of blue, black, red, and yellow—across the roofs to dry. Boys and men watched for enemies who might come to steal the corn. If anyone approached, men quickly pulled up the ladders people used to get in and out of their hillside homes.

Although large game were not plentiful here, boys learned to hunt. Occasionally, men could trap or kill a deer, which was shot with bows and arrows. On hunting parties, older Hopi boys learned to form a circle around the deer, then shoot at the same time.

Navajo boys learned how to make pitfall traps along deer trails by digging pits, then hiding the holes with vegetation. They also learned to catch rabbits with nets woven from brush (later, from cotton cord). On the prairie, boys captured prairie dogs, a member of the squirrel family. They dug the animals out of their burrows or shot them with bows and arrows. Hunters asked an animal's forgiveness before killing it.

Young Yuma boys living along the lower Colorado River became skillful fishermen. They used long fishing poles, with cotton lines and hooks made from the curved spines of a cactus plant.

Children also spent a great deal of time gathering food. Taos girls collected pine nuts from the mountain slopes, knocking them from the trees with long poles. They were careful not to take more than was needed, so as not to deprive squirrels and other creatures. Acorns were important to the Western Apache. They were eaten plain or ground into flour to be mixed with soup or sprinkled on foods.

A large cactus called agave (century plant) was important to desert people. They could roast and eat its crown and

These young Hopi women are grinding corn on metates, a skill all must learn before marriage. Their hairstyles show that they are unmarried; after marriage, Hopi women braided their hair.

flowers and make its juice into drinks. The rest of the agave was used, too. Thorns served as needles, fiber from the leaves was used as thread, and the stalks made shafts for spears and fiddles played by Apache men.

The Pima ate the fruit of the saguaro, another cactus. The fruits were used to make dried cakes and boiled into syrup to store for winter. Children ate toasted saguaro seeds, which also were ground and mixed with water to make mush. The annual saguaro feast was an important rain-making ceremony for the Pima.

Working with their mothers, girls learned how to prepare food. Younger girls fetched drinking and cooking water in *ollas,* large pots they learned to balance on their heads. When girls reached their teens, they knew more than fifty ways to cook corn. They spent hours each day grinding corn against a *metate,* a stone with an indented surface, with a handheld stone called a *mano.*

Girls practiced making *piki* bread. With their fingers, they spread the dough, made of cornmeal and water, on a hot, lightly greased stone. As they finished cooking, the piki were removed and rolled up, then placed in a basket. There were burnt fingers along the way as girls became adept at making thin, flaky piki.

Instead of piki, Navajo girls made fry bread, a staple food among their people. As sheepherders, the Navajo also included more meat dishes in their diet and cooked meat-based stews and soups.

Games and Recreation

Even with so much work to do, there was still time to play or visit friends. Very young children liked to chase butterflies and birds, as children have done for centuries. Four- and five-year-olds competed in special races in which they kicked a ball as they ran along. Players were allowed to move the ball only with their feet, even running over areas with thorns or cactus.

Hopi children played with tops made by the men in the tribe. Boys' tops were painted with bands of red, white, or black, while girls had plain ones. Besides being playthings, tops had spiritual significance and were thought to bring the wind. Rules limited the times of year when tops could be used. They were banned after early spring, a time when harsh winds could damage crops.

The Navajo also had a "wind" toy, a whirligig made of a thin piece of wood with a cord attached to one end. Children twirled the toys around their head to make a roaring noise. The tribe viewed the toy as a thunderbird.

At night, older Hopi and Pueblo boys played "witch-hunt." A boy with a drum, called the witch, would hide. If players were searching in the wrong place, he beat on the drum, then ran to a new hiding place before they could find him.

Women and girls sometimes played games of chance or skill. In one game, a player juggled four stones while walking toward a goal. She tried to reach that spot without dropping any stones.

The ring game, played with a hoop and darts, was popular both in the Southwest and the Plains. Players rolled a hoop along the ground as fast as possible while opponents tried to throw darts through it. Hopi boys used a hoop woven of corn husks (called a *we-la*) and a dart with feathers *(ma-te-va)*. In order to count their darts at the end, each player used a different color.

Coming of Age

Elaborate ceremonies marked the coming of age of young adults. Preparing for such solemn ceremonies, they might wash their hair with special shampoo made from the yucca plant. Hopi young people carried an ear of corn, the same sacred ear that had been laid beside them when they were born.

Before turning seventeen, a Hopi girl had to show her skill during a four-day corn-grinding ceremony. She then earned the right to wear a special hairdo that resembled butterfly wings. This hairstyle showed that the girl was ready for marriage.

When a Tohono O'odham (Papago) girl reached adolescence, blue lines were tattooed on her face with a cactus thorn. A Tohono O'odham (Papago) boy had to run long distances across the desert until he was exhausted and the

A woman arranges the hair of an unmarried Hopi girl in the elaborate squash blossom style, a sign that she is now ready for marriage.

image of an animal came to him—a type of vision quest like that undertaken by Plains Indians.

Upon reaching adulthood, a Zuni boy could at last have a mask of his own instead of borrowing one for ceremonial dances. After marriage, he hung this mask in his home, and it was buried with him when he died.

Chiricahua Apache boys spent much time preparing to become warriors and might join their first battle by age seventeen. They went into the wilderness to learn survival skills. One test required them to run four miles carrying a mouthful of water which they should not swallow until the end.

Navajo initiation rites were held for both boys and girls during an annual nine-day Night Chant ceremony. To launch girls into puberty, the Navajo performed the *kinaalda,* a group of ceremonies that is part of the Blessing Way. The many rites that make up the Blessing Way mark significant events in Navajo life. The *kinaalda* reenacted the original coming of age of Changing Woman, daughter of First Man and First Woman. The Navajo believed that during the ceremony, the young girl actually became Changing Woman. The ceremony, with its special prayers, songs, and ritual corn-grinding, was meant to protect the girl from evil and promote *hozho*—beauty, harmony, and goodness, the basic Navajo values.

Apache girls took part in an elaborate four-day, four-night ceremony. Before it began, the girl was dressed carefully in a fine dress made of buckskin, dyed golden yellow to resemble pollen. The sponsoring "godmother" decorated her cheeks with pollen. The girl was then called by the name White-Painted Woman, "mother of all Apache," and was thought to have special powers during the rituals. Her godmother led her through the Sunrise Dance Ceremony, which is still held today. This same woman would remain close to the girl all their lives.

At night, male singers performed special songs meant to guide the girl toward a healthy, productive life. After the first night, one singer painted himself and the girl with designs that had a religious significance. The girl walked along a path marked with holy pollen to symbolize a long, happy life.

On the fourth and last night, a holy man blessed the young woman, saying, "the sun . . . has come down to the Earth; It has come to her. . . . Long life! Its power is good." Then the girl and her female attendant separated from the group for four days. When she returned to her parents' tepee, she was ready for marriage.

Whatever the tribe, coming-of-age customs aimed to connect young people with the gods. Spiritual leaders reminded the young people, "We shall be as one person," that is, humans united with the spirit world. For Indians in the Southwest, these words formed a bridge between youth and adulthood, an echo of the words they had heard during the religious ceremonies of their childhood.

Chapter Four

Growing Up on the Plains

March had come to the Great Plains, and a group of Sioux boys headed for the woods with their bows and arrows. Now that warm weather had arrived, they might find game. Several boys imitated the sounds of a chipmunk while the others hid behind trees, waiting. As dozens of chipmunks ran over the snow, the boys began shooting arrows at them.

While the buffalo was the mainstay for the Plains hunting tribes, a boy could not join buffalo hunts until he was about thirteen years old. Young boys could practice their skills and find food for their villages by hunting rabbits, squirrels, and other small prey.

Indians living on the Plains included the Sioux and other great hunting tribes—the Shoshone, Kutenai, Blackfoot, Crow, Arapaho, Assiniboine, Cheyenne, Comanche, and Kiowa. With scant rainfall, the western plains were not suited for farming, so these groups wandered about in search of game.

The eastern prairie had more rain and better land for farming. The Indians who lived there—the Arikara, Hidatsa, Kansa, Mandan, Osage, Omaha, Pawnee, and Wichita—were both hunters and farmers who had permanent villages. The territory inhabited by these groups stretched across the central portion of the present-day United States, from the Mississippi River to the Rocky Mountains.

Homes and Villages

The broad, grass-covered midwestern plains of North America held numerous land animals, large and small—elk, buffalo, deer, antelope, sheep, mountain goats, prairie dogs, coyotes, wolves, bobcats, bears, and foxes. Beaver and fish inhabited the waters, while eagles and other birds swooped across the skies. A hunting people, the Plains Indians faced many challenges as they struggled to meet their basic needs and to remain safe from feared enemies.

Most Plains villages were of tepees fashioned from buffalo hides. Tepees could be moved during different seasons of the year as the band moved about to hunt or escape harsh weather. Villages were typically busy and friendly, and people enjoyed visiting each other. Children soon learned the rules: An open tepee flap meant that visitors were welcome. If the flap was closed, visitors must ask permission to enter. People who did not want visitors placed two crossed sticks over the entrance of their tepee.

Children in prairie farmer groups, such as the Osage, lived in extended families, sometimes in a wooden lodge rather than a tepee. Children might belong to either their mother's or father's clan. In winter, a Mandan child might awaken in a spacious lodge that housed the family's horse and dogs as well. For furnishings, the Mandans used fur mats and backrests made of reeds. Clothing and moccasins, wet with snow, were hung on wooden bars in the sun.

A group of tepees at Wind River in Wyoming, about 1870. The tepee with painted symbols belonged to the great Shoshone chief Washakie (Shoots-the-Buffalo-Running).

Spirituality and Legends

From the moment of birth, spirituality was part of daily life. A holy man in a Plains village might fast before celebrating a birth. At the ceremony, he held up the infant in its cradleboard, asking the Great Spirit to guide the newborn all of his or her life. The holy man might also ask that when death came, the person's hair would be "white like the snows on the mountaintops." Then he gave the infant a name to be used in childhood. For Sioux George Eastman (Ohiyesa), this name was Hakadah—"the pitiful last." He was the last-born of five children whose mother died soon after his birth. His adult name, Ohiyesa, meant "winner."

Everyone in the tribe assembled for the annual Sun Dance, meant to ensure a successful buffalo hunt. Every part of the ceremony had a special meaning. Listening, children learned a great deal about their history and the importance of the buffalo.

While most boys would become hunters and warriors, some were groomed for the role of shaman—prophet and healer. Holy men learned tribal myths, legends, prayers, and songs, as well as the ceremonial rites and dances. Healers learned various curing rites and the uses of herbs and plant substances during illness. Most shamans were men, but in some hunting tribes, such as the Sioux, women also served as healers. Older women, regarded as quite wise, might become religious advisers or counselors.

Childhood

Among the Osage, babies were viewed as small stars from the Spiritland in the sky. Their first cries were prayers to Grandfather the Sun, prayers they learned before being born on Earth. A baby's naming ceremony took place as dawn reddened the sky, a sacred time to the Osage. At age ten, children received two formal adult names, one for the sky and one for the Earth.

Plains babies learned to be rugged. When a male Sioux was born, the older siblings had to plunge him naked into the water or roll him in the snow if it was winter. A new warrior had been born, and he must prepare for the strenuous life ahead.

Cheyenne babies sometimes received a gift of moccasins at birth, with two holes deliberately cut on their soles. It was believed that if Death came to take the baby, it would see the holes and leave the child alone, since one could not embark on a long journey with worn-out moccasins.

A Kiowa woman and her child, strapped into its cradleboard. The rounded frame around the top protected the child's head in case the board tipped forward.

Plains babies rested in wooden cradleboards covered with soft animal skins. Many boards had embroidered sacks nailed to one side, laced with buckskin strings. Babies could play with carved bones, hooves, and other objects attached to the side of the cradleboard. While working outdoors, the mothers hung the boards from wild grape vines or other flexible branches. A breeze might rock her child, or a bird entertain the baby with its songs and nimble movements.

At the annual Sun Dance held by many tribes, a special ceremony took place when the ears of babies between the ages of three and six months were pierced. A highly respected warrior sat in a lodge and conducted the piercing as each baby was brought forward, lying in a beaded bag on his or her cradleboard. Decorative rings were then placed in the ears.

Young children were told not to make noises that could draw enemies to the camp or scare away buffalo. Walking through the woods, they learned how to step softly, without cracking a twig or moving fallen leaves or stray pebbles.

Children were not spoiled but were seldom punished. They learned independence and useful skills. Boys and girls learned how to ride horses and shoot a bow and arrow and use a knife. All had to know how to defend themselves in an emergency.

There was work for everyone. Young girls fetched water or gathered wood or buffalo chips for fires. Older girls helped with household chores, child care, and food gathering. They helped build and decorate buffalo skin tepees and made tools and utensils. They also did plain and fancy sewing and crafted jewelry, armbands, and headbands, often embellishing them with beautiful embroidery.

Boys learned hunting, fishing, trapping, weapon-making, and other jobs performed by men. They aimed to become expert horsemen. Blackfoot boys joined the men for daily morning swims, even in cold weather. After breakfast (usually boiled meat), they helped the men round up the horses. Older boys joined hunting parties, while small ones played sports designed to build their strength.

As they neared their teens, boys often tried to join a war or hunting party before their family had given permission. Those who sneaked off to join the older men might make themselves useful by gathering firewood or water or doing other tasks for the group.

When George Eastman (Ohiyesa) returned from a day outdoors, his grandfather would ask him many questions,

The dresses of these two Comanche girls show the creativity and artistry involved in bead and leatherwork.

sometimes for an hour or more: "On which side of the trees is the lighter-colored bark? On which side do they have the most regular branches? How do you know that there are fish in yonder lake?"[1] Eastman later wrote,

> It was his custom to let me name all the new birds I had seen during the day. I would name them according to the color or the shape of their bill or their song or the appearance and locality of the nest—in fact anything about the bird that impressed me as characteristic . . .[2]

Providing Food

Meat, the main food for Plains Indians, came mostly from the buffalo. These animals also yielded skins for clothing and tepees, fur for robes, and bones for tools and utensils. No part of the animal would go unused.

A successful hunt meant surviving the winter. Young men looked forward to killing a buffalo, something that required courage and skill. Lieutenant Frederic Ruxton, an army officer who lived on the Plains during the 1840s, said, "No animal requires so much killing as the buffalo. Unless shot through the lungs or spine, they usually escape."[3]

Among prairie farmer groups like the Osage, children learned more domestic chores. By about age ten, a girl could cook, tend crops, and make clothing. Like a girl on the Plains, she learned to scrape and tan buffalo hides. Children also helped to gather wild plant foods—chokecherries, berries, seeds, edible bulbs, roots, and small birds' eggs. In farming prairie groups the roles of girls and boys were similar.

Meals often began with a prayer of thanks, after which the men were served, then the women and the children. If food was scarce, grownups often gave their portion to the

A YOUNG MAN'S FIRST BUFFALO HUNT

"When I was ten years old in Indian Territory [present-day Oklahoma, the region to which the U.S. government forcibly moved many Indians during the 1800s], I commenced to kill buffalo calves, killing them with bows and arrows, and then when I grew up about fourteen years old, I had killed big buffalo good many," recalled the Cheyenne leader Roman Nose.[6]

Black Elk, an Oglala Sioux, recalls that a hunt started when the crier rode into the village shouting, "Many bison, I hear! They are coming, they are coming; Your children, you must take care of them!"[7] Black Elk describes the trip to follow the herd: "We broke camp and started in formation, the four advisers first, a crier behind them, the chiefs next, and then the people with the loaded pony drags in a long line, and the herd of ponies following. I was riding near the rear with some of the smaller boys . . ."[8]

Horses were trained to ride alongside the moving buffalo without being steered by the rider. Drawing close, the buffalo hunter aimed his arrow toward the animal's left shoulder. Often, it took two or three arrows to hit vital organs and kill the buffalo.

Standing Bear, a Minneconjou Sioux, joined some hunts before age thirteen and managed to kill a young buffalo, or calf. The July he turned thirteen, Standing Bear joined the hunt as a man for the first time. When he managed to shoot a yearling, he let out a triumphant cry of "Yuhoo!" in the traditional way.[9]

A young man returning from his first hunt earned high praise. His father might even hold a feast in his honor and distribute gifts to needy villagers. Women praised his courage in song.

children. The Plains diet—meat and some wild plants in season—was enhanced with maple sugar, which some Sioux bands in present-day Minnesota made. Children also liked a tasty white sugar made from the box-elder tree.

Games and Recreation

To children living on the Great Plains of the American West, the arrival of the warm seasons was a time of great rejoicing. With horses and wide open spaces, they enjoyed much freedom. According to Sioux George Eastman,

> During the summer, when Nature is at her best, and provides abundantly . . . it seems to me that no life is happier than [an Indian's]! Food is free—lodging free—everything free! All were alike rich in the summer, and again, all were alike poor in the winter and early spring. . . . The Indian boy enjoyed such a life as almost all boys dream of and would choose for themselves if they were permitted to do so.[4]

In between chores, children played games and enjoyed handmade toys. Until age seven or eight, boys and girls played together near their mothers. Their toys might include dolls or model tepees. Boys had miniature bows, arrows, and shields. A young boy might be able to kill a rabbit with one of his toy weapons. Both girls and boys played with toys shaped like important animals—buffalo, elk, and bears. Some played musical instruments or enjoyed singing.

Sioux boys liked to toss a hoop into the air. Other players tried to catch it on a forked pole as it descended. Mandan children played a game in which they threw darts through a rolling hoop. Women and children especially liked a game called *shinny*, which resembles today's field hockey. This energetic game was played with sticks that curved slightly at the end and a ball about the size of a baseball.

There were also pets. Mandans loved dogs, and often shared their homes with them. George Eastman described some of the pets he and his friends had as children:

> We had many curious wild pets. There were young foxes, bears, wolves, raccoons, fawns, buffalo calves, and birds of all kinds, tamed by various boys. My pets were different at different times, but I particularly remember one. I once had a grizzly bear for a pet and so far as he and I were concerned, our relations were charming and very close.[5]

Blackfoot children enjoyed miniature tepees made from the leaves of the cottonwood tree. Their legends said that the idea for a tepee dwelling had come from an Indian ancestor who had been twisting the cottonwood leaf around in his hand one day.

A time when children needed toys to amuse themselves quietly was during trips to the buffalo camp. While moving along with a caravan of people, a girl might play with her favorite doll while sitting on the wood platform of a travois—two poles lashed together in an A-shape, then attached to a horse's saddle. While on the move, a boy might try to quiet the family dog.

On these trips, girls might be lucky enough to find or receive elk teeth. They would later use their collection of teeth to adorn their best dress. Only two teeth from a single elk could be used, and a dress required about 300. The dress was a possession she cherished all her life.

Coming of Age

Adolescent boys and girls took on more responsibility, according to their talents. Boys learned more advanced skills for hunting and warfare, as well as how to take part in tribal government. At council meetings, people discussed matters that concerned the tribe and tried to agree about how to handle problems. Black Elk recalled that as a child, he was often curious about what the men were doing inside the council tepee.

As Plains girls grew up, they were taught to be dignified and composed, rejecting the giggling or silly ways of younger years. To accomplish this, a Blackfoot father sat down with his daughter and told her funny stories, encouraging her to laugh a lot. He repeated these stories over and over for days until the girl was able to sit calmly. Then he praised her for behaving well.

Just as girls of today enjoy their dollhouses, Sioux girls on the Plains liked playing with miniature tepees.

A young Blackfoot girl wearing her prized elk-tooth dress.

When they reached their early teens, boys and girls took part in coming-of-age ceremonies. For some boys, the rituals began with a visit to the sweat lodge. Sweating was thought to remove impurities from the body. After drinking a great deal of water, the boy sat naked in a hut with his helper. The walls were splashed with water that turned to steam as hot rocks were placed along the walls.

After that, the young man embarked on a solitary journey to a hilltop. There he found a place near a tree or rock and sat in a hole. Fasting, with only a buffalo hide for warmth, he waited for the vision of an animal spirit to come to him. The quest might take three or four days and nights. From the animal seen in the vision came the boy's adult name.

Some boys had a vision of thunder, and they were called *heyoka*—"backwards-forwards man." This meant the boy must shave one side of his head, and on the other side, let his hair hang down to his waist. Heyokas were thought to have magical powers to cure the sick, make predictions, and help their people.

Girls did not embark on a vision quest, but their coming of age was just as important. A girl who was physically ready to become a mother was the guest of honor at a feast given by her parents. She received new clothing, and relatives sang her praises before a circle of well-wishers. During these times, young people received much advice and heard the wise words that had been passed on for generations: "See the world not only with your two eyes, but also with the one eye that is in your heart."

Chapter Five

Growing Up in the Far West

The cry of a newborn infant pierced the quiet darkness of the desert night. It was Paiute country, in what is now Nevada, during the early 1700s. Hearing the sound, the Paiute father raced up into the hills as fast as his legs could carry him. This tradition was meant to guarantee that his child would have strong legs, strength needed for the hard life that lay ahead.

The Paiute, like other Great Basin groups, were always on the move. They had no crops to harvest and not much large game available for food. To survive, they must find whatever food they could in their dry lands.

In addition to the Paiute, other tribes of the Great Basin were the Ute, Gosiute, Northern Paiute (Paviotso), Shoshone, Washo, Bannock, and Mono. They lived in present-day Nevada and Utah, as well as parts of Oregon, Idaho, Wyoming, Colorado, and California.

To the north, living in a more hospitable region, in what are now Oregon, Idaho, and Washington State, lived the

Columbia Plateau tribes: Nez Perce, Kutenai (Flathead), Yakima, Cayuse, Columbia, Wenatchee, and Coeur d'Alene.

To the south, in present-day California, were the Modoc, Hupa, Yurok, Pomo, Miwok, Wintun, Maidu, Chumash, and Yokut Indians.

Homes and Villages

The Great Basin was a harsh region in which to live. People lived in small groups; usually a few families set up camp together. Since food was scarce, they moved about to find it during various seasons, living in caves or movable shelters made of brush and tree limbs. However, Great Basin people lived without much fear of war or attacks from neighboring tribes, since they did not have land or possessions others wanted.

The Columbia Plateau region is a place of rugged beauty. Snowcapped mountains rise above winding rivers, lush valleys, and deep canyons. The rivers are home to salmon and other fish that have sustained generations since ancient times.

On the Plateau, children lived in long communal lodges that might house as many as thirty families. They slept on reed mats woven from bulrushes, cattails, and other plant fibers. In winter, families often moved to pit houses, circular in shape and built over deep pits dug in the ground. Dirt was piled up around the sides of the houses to help keep out the cold, bitter winds.

Indians living in what is now California enjoyed a mild or warm climate with plentiful natural resources. From the ocean came a bounty of food. Edible plants, seeds, and nuts were available, and crops could be grown. In this climate, the Pomo built tepees shaped like cones and covered with willows and rushes. Some houses in this region were built partially underground. Village meeting houses were built in a central location.

The Chumash and Yokuts lived in round brush houses shaped like domes. When a home was being built, children helped the women of the tribe gather tule reed from nearby marshes. The women wove the reeds into mats, then used them to cover the pole frame of the house. Chumash children slept in small beds tucked under the larger ones of their parents.

Spirituality and Legends

Prayers for guidance, help, and thanksgiving were part of daily life in this region, as in other Native American cultures. Children in the Plateau and Great Basin heard many tales about Coyote, the spirit helper of Haniyawaat, the Creator who had made all things. Coyote was capable of both good and mischief. While listening to these tales, children could think about the struggle between good and evil and the importance of choosing good.

Coyote appeared in the creation story told among the Nez Perce. A large, ravenous beast had eaten many animals, then ate Coyote, too. He managed to escape from the monster's stomach and cut out its heart. When he cut its body into pieces and threw them around, the first people on Earth were created. A site in present-day Idaho was viewed as the sacred location of this event.

At the end of the evening, dinner signaled storytime in many tribes. Mothers and grandmothers might tell the stories. Bedtime came when the last embers of the fire had died. All the children were expected to observe carefully and learn the songs, dances, and rituals of their people taught by example and through oral history.

Childhood

Like Indian babies in other regions, those in the tribes of the Far West spent their first months attached to cradleboards. Rabbit skins kept some lucky babies warm in winter. Babies were freed from time to time so they could crawl, then walk and play on the ground. Those old enough to walk spent time playing with other children.

The Yuroks of present-day northern California marked a girl's age by tattooing. At age five, a black line was made from each ear to her chin. A new black line was added every five years.

As they grew, Plateau children were reared by grandparents as well as parents. They were not sternly disciplined but rather guided toward correct behavior. The scorn of their fellow villagers steered children away from misdeeds more than the fear of physical punishment.

Chores kept children busy throughout the year. Boys learned to fish, hunt, and build and operate a canoe. Girls learned to make clothing, care for the younger children, keep house, and gather and prepare food.

Native American girls in California helped their mothers care for children, strapping the babies on their backs if they were big enough. They began learning to weave baskets at an early age, starting with simple ones and learning more and more complicated designs and techniques. Some consider the baskets of these groups, especially the Pomo, to be the finest made today in the United States. Over the centuries, the Pomo developed expert methods of weaving and coiling. They took great care in selecting grasses, roots, and stems for their baskets. Plant dyes made of berry juice, mud, and trees were used to color the materials.

Spending time with their fathers, Chumash and Pomo boys learned to make small tools and bows and fishhooks for

Joseppa Beatty, a famous Central Pomo-speaking basketmaker, shown here in 1892 at Yokayo Ranchero with her husband and son.

hunting and fishing. They learned to aim a curved stick at rabbits and other small game to kill them and learned how to skin the animals. Boys climbed trees in search of birds' eggs and ran a great deal to build up their strength.

Like their counterparts on the Pacific coast, Plateau boys learned to be good fishermen. From May through November each year, millions of salmon rushed through the rivers and mountain streams in their region. Trout, sturgeon, and other fish were plentiful. A hard-working, skillful boy could catch them with traps laid across a stream or with lines and hooks, spears, or bows and arrows.

Ornate Styles of Dress

Coastal tribes had access to more food throughout the year and gained wealth through trading dried fish and seashells. This gave them more time to spend on arts and crafts, such as basket-weaving, and on their appearance. Girls in southern California took great care with their hair. Chumash women liked to cut bangs across their foreheads. They wore hairpins made of bone and sometimes conditioned their hair with mesquite gum mixed with clay. This mixture was left on for days, then washed out, leaving the hair quite shiny.

This picture, taken about 1900, shows Coos Bay children wearing traditional rain capes made of plant fibers.

Many girls living in warm climates also decorated their hair with flowers.

In warm climates children wore no clothing until adolescence. At that time girls began to dress like their mothers, and boys wore animal skins around their hips as their fathers did. In cold climates, people used deerskin blankets at night and wore them as capes in the daytime during the cold months.

Women and girls also wore fringed skirts made of animal skins. The fringe made it easier for them to sit and work, as when they ground acorns into meal. They wore ornaments of shells and beads around their waists, wrists, and necks. Some also designed hairbands and belts of bright-colored birds' feathers and shells. When carrying heavy baskets on their heads, they wore tightly woven caps, also decorated.

Finding Food

Finding enough food to survive consumed most of the day for people who lived in the Great Basin. Children worked side by side with adults to ensure the family's survival. Families kept on the move, first in order to find water. Then they gathered whatever wild foods they could find—rice grass, wild barley, dropseed, pickleweed, and nuts. Boys caught fish and turtles from the few lakes in their region. They also captured mice, lizards, grasshoppers, and large crickets for meals.

Girls looked for bird and duck eggs and gathered edible roots and bulbs from the ground, as well as nuts, seeds, and whatever else they could find. These were eaten during the warm months and carefully stored for the lean winters.

The Paiute, Shoshone, and Gosiute formed large groups only for major game hunts and gathering times, such as the pinyon nut harvest. The trees, which grew at an altitude of about 7,000 feet (2,134 meters) along the mountains, yielded nuts only in certain years. To harvest them, Indians used long sticks to knock cones containing nuts from the pinyon trees. Nuts were roasted and stored.

Plateau families also did not raise crops but, instead, gathered edible wild foods that grew in their region. Each summer the Nez Perce camped on what is now called Camas Prairie. Nez Perce women and girls moved about the prairie, which was carpeted with bright blue flowers of the camas, a bulb plant belonging to the lily family. These flowers were not only a thing of beauty to the Nez Perce and other Indians living in the Far West, they were a mainstay of their diet, year-round.

Bending toward the ground, girls used long curved sticks made from willow branches to dig up the bulbs. The starchy camas bulbs were ground into meal, some to be saved, some to make into delicious cakes for eating right away. Besides savoring the taste of fresh camas cakes, children renewed friendships with young people from other bands who had come to harvest the bulbs. They played games, and shared news of the past year.

Besides camas, there were edible roots, wild carrots and onions, currants, herbs, and nuts on the prairie. Girls gathered roots and berries from the forests on the coast—cranberries, blueberries, and the saskatoon berry, which was very nutritious.

The Nez Perce did not make clay objects. Cooking in the Plateau region was done in watertight baskets made of cedar roots.

Indians in California enjoyed many edible wild plants throughout the year—seeds, roots, fruits, and nuts. There were cresses, celery, acorns, and bulbs that could be ground to make flour. Sources of protein included meat from bears and from the various kinds of fish and seafood—crabs, shrimp, whitefish, sardines, river trout, and turtles from their waters.

On some occasions, gathering wild food plants was like a family vacation. Chumash families packed their mats and went to a special area, usually the mountains or hills, where seeds and nuts were plentiful. They filled their baskets with enough berries, edible bulbs, and herbs to last until the next year.

Games and Recreation

Nez Perce children enjoyed games using items they found around them. A favorite of young children was the pinecone game, played with a hoop made from willow branches or long reeds. Children stood some distance from the hoop, which lay on the ground, and aimed pinecones at it. The game was made more challenging as players moved farther from the hoop or set new rules about how one could throw—underhand or overhand, for instance. Players could earn more points if their cones landed in certain parts of the hoop.

Another popular pastime was a mud fight called "flipper," in which boys threw mud balls from the end of sticks at the other team. People also played tug-of-war, with boys and men teaming up against women and girls. Young boys played with miniature bows and arrows; girls usually had dolls and tiny cradles. Often, these dolls were pieces of deerskin on a stick or were fashioned of dried mud or grass.

Coming of Age

Eventually, the more carefree days of childhood made way for the passage to adult life. As they reached adolescence, coastal boys and girls hoped to have a vision of an animal helper or spirit to guide them through life. Throughout

A VISION QUEST IN THE PLATEAU

Around age ten, a child from the Nez Perce or other Plateau tribe might embark on a vision quest. The purpose of this solitary journey was to seek a spirit guardian who would bestow spirit power, or *weeyekin,* on the recipient all his or her life. The spirit might take the form of a bear, owl, elk, eagle, antelope, snake, or other animal. Spirit help could aid men in battle or during the hunt or enable a person to become a healer.

As the child set out alone, an adult tied a sacred object, such as a feather, to a piece of his or her clothing. In the mountains, the child built a fire, which could not be allowed to die out. The child began to pray and fast as the sun set, then continued to face the same direction until the sun rose once again the next morning. At that point, the child turned to face the dawn. This same pattern, with continued fasting, was repeated the next night and day. If all went well, the child received a vision of the animal helper spirit during this period.

Meanwhile, back in the village, the parents prepared a feast for their child's return. During the feast, shared with family and friends, nobody asked the child to discuss his or her experiences. It was thought that talking about the vision might reduce its power. By the age of fifteen, the young person might have undertaken several such quests, in the hopes of forging a strong connection to the spirit world.

childhood, they were given training to prepare for such a vision. Boys who had received a vision were given special songs and were allowed to use the cry of their helper animal.

Boys had their growing-up ceremonies at age fourteen or fifteen. In several tribes, young men drank a special preparation made with jimsonweed, a powerful plant that could kill someone who drank too much. In the amounts used, the drink led to visions or dreams, and a boy felt drowsy after drinking it. When he roused and shared the dream he had experienced, older men sang and gave him advice about how to view the world and behave as an adult male.

If they had not done so already, young men turning eighteen would look for wives. They were told that the most important quality in a future wife was that she be hard-working and skilled at making baskets and gathering food. These traits were seen as more valuable than a girl's appearance.

In order to marry, a young Yurok man needed to have a string of rare seashells (called dentalium) the length of his arm to present to his bride. After the marriage, their own first-born son would receive the shells—a family heirloom to bestow on his own bride and to be passed down for generations to come.

Chapter Six

Growing Up on the Northwest Coast

One summer in the early 1800s, a group of Indians gathered on the beach of what is now called Puget Sound. The first salmon of the year had been spotted, a time of rejoicing for people of all ages. Barefoot children played, darting in and out of the water, while grownups smiled at the fish streaming in the waters.

Although salmon was the chief food for tribes living on the Northwest Coast, they also had an abundance of other foods. In May, when the tides were low, they dug for butterclams in the sand. Game could be found in their forests; wild fruits and vegetables grew in and around the forests. They enjoyed more natural resources than any other group on the continent.

Living on the coast that stretched for 2,000 miles (3,219 kilometers) along the Pacific Ocean from southern Alaska to Northern California were a number of important tribes: the

Bella Coola, Chinook, Haida, Klikitat, Kwakiutl, Coast Salish, Nootka, Quileute, Quinault, Tlingit, and Tsimshian.

Homes and Villages

Surrounded by forests, the Northwest Indians had a rich supply of wood available for homes, as well as for canoes, masks, and totem poles. Coastal Indians built spacious gabled plank houses, usually of red cedar, where wealthier families lived in winter. Several families could live in one large plank house. Plainer plank sheds provided the year-round housing for less wealthy members of the tribe, as well as summer homes for the wealthy, or nobles. Nobles lived in such sheds only in the summer. Since carving was the main art among these people, house posts and door poles were carved and painted with the family symbols.

Most children lived in extended families that included three generations or more. Several such groups, living near each other, made up a village. The man living in the largest home, who would be the wealthiest villager, was usually chosen as leader, called a chieftain. Chiefs were at the top of Northwest Indian society, followed by nobles, commoners, and finally, slaves. People were born into their class, whether noble or commoner. Slaves were often people who had been defeated in battle.

These people made fine canoes, some 60 feet (18 meters) long. Ornate carvings decorated many canoes. Young people learned to steer these vessels through the rivers, streams, lakes, and coastal waters.

Spirituality and Legends

Here, as in other regions, animal figures were an important part of spiritual life. Among the Haida, it was believed that people could be changed into animals. One legend said that an adopted boy named Sin was later shown to be a sky god, at which time he transformed himself into a woodpecker.

Spiritual leaders called medicine men had high status within the tribes. Some were invited to come to other villages to help people deal with trouble and would arrive in a canoe that was specially decorated with spiritual symbols. They used ivory charms carved with ornate designs during their ceremonies.

Animal symbols could also be seen in the carvings on totem poles. Totem means "family" or "clan," and the totems told the stories of the family and clan. They were also made as memorial poles to the dead and as grave posts. When a new totem was to be carved, great care was taken to select the right tree. It must be located near enough to water to be transported back to the village. Some designs, such as eyes and ears, were made from patterns so they would be the same on each side. Figures on totems included beavers, eagles, sharks, ravens, toads, and bears. Black paint was made from charcoal, and white was made from baked clamshells. A certain clay mixed with fish oil yielded yellow, and shades of red came from berries and roots.

Childhood

Among these tribes, a baby was thought to be a deceased relative on the mother's side of the family, reborn. A new baby and its mother stayed in a bark shelter away from other people until the child was ten days old.

Babies in the Northwest had wooden cradles, usually carved from cedar logs and lined with dried moss. Some cradles were carved to resemble canoes. After being bathed, babies were dried with shredded cedar bark and rubbed with whale oil before being strapped into their cradles.

Canoes, resting on a beach in 1878, were a major form of transportation for people in the Northwest. The animal and bird designs on the totems had important spiritual meanings.

Babies wore diapers made from shredded cedar bark, which was also used to make the padding for their cradleboards. Cedar bark was also used to make plates, sitting mats, and sleeping mats. Babies played with rattles and strings of beads made from shells. Among the southern tribes, the babies' heads were bound to make their foreheads taper upward and back.

Parents also pinched boys' noses and pulled them in a downward position so they would grow long and straight, considered an asset among the northwestern peoples. A protruding lower lip was considered beautiful for women of the Tlingit and Haida groups. The lips of baby girls were pierced with a thin piece of sinew, and a piece of shell was added as the girls grew older. A piece of wood called a labret was placed inside the lower lip to make it stick out. All children wore necklaces and earrings made of shells.

Children might be nursed until they were two or three years old. Older babies also ate fish broth and mashed fish.

At about age six, children of the Northwest Coast received their names. At a simple ceremony, the village chief held the child in his arms while dancing in a circle, at the same time chanting the child's new name. Children's ears might be pierced at this time.

When boys were about seven, they went to live in the home of their mother's brother (their uncle), who was responsible for rearing him. Through daily exercises, chores, and having to take morning baths in icy water, boys were taught to be brave and to withstand discomfort. During these years, they learned about the history of their clan and family and the traditions of the tribe.

Girls learned their domestic duties as they worked with their mothers. They gathered wild foods and helped to make clothing, kitchen tools, and blankets for the home. They also learned to make and decorate the cone-shaped hats with wide brims that people wore on ceremonial occasions. They wove watertight baskets and carrying bags from spruce roots. Bark could be cut and twisted to make into rope or cord.

In the Tlingit tribe, girls learned how to weave beautiful and colorful blankets. They were made of fibers from cedar bark and the hair of mountain goats. Colors included greenish blue, yellow, and black, obtained from plants and roots.

The blankets were a sign of wealth and were worn on special occasions.

Finding Food

Since seafood and fish were so abundant, northwestern children did not fear starvation. They also did not have to spend time in the fields planting, growing, or tending crops as Indian children did in some other regions.

Girls gathered edible wild foods such as nuts, berries, roots, and wild carrots and onions, and they gathered clams and other shellfish from the shore. They also learned to clean and dry the fish that were caught by the men and boys of the tribe.

Girls spent many hours berry picking, since blueberries, currants, and salmonberries were plentiful. As the older girls and women shook the bushes, young ones picked up fallen berries from the ground.

Boys learned the important task of salmon fishing. Salmon were caught in various ways—with nets made of plant fibers, with spears, or with bows and arrows. By paddling out into the water in their canoes, the boys could use these different methods of catching salmon as the salmon moved along the stream on their annual summer journey.

During the summer, villages of people followed the salmon, camping on islands or in certain bays where fishing was good. In the camps, they built brush shelters and slept on piles of twigs covered with fur robes, blankets, or mats. They also hunted seals, sea lions, and sea otters.

Some salmon were eaten fresh, but a great amount were dried on long wooden tables for use throughout the year. A thanksgiving ceremony marked the annual salmon harvest. Villagers of all ages helped to clean, split, and dry the fish, then hang them up to dry. Dried fish were stored in baskets and boxes.

Games and Recreation

Boys imitated the fishing and hunting skills of their elders, playing with toy harpoons. They learned to spear fish as they played in the water. Boys also used pieces of sharp shells to whittle sticks and pieces of food, learning these skills from watching craftsmen in their villages. On the beach, they scratched designs in the wet sand. Some boys might grow up to be expert carvers, highly respected in their tribes.

Competing with each other, boys enjoyed foot races and wrestling games. Using smaller-sized sets of bows and arrows, they took part in arrow-shooting contests to see who could hit the targets the most often.

Girls played with toy mats, dishes, blankets, and carved wooden dolls. Some of their playtime was devoted to pretending to be different animals that lived around them. Girls also enjoyed swimming and playing on the seashore and learned to paddle small canoes, as did the boys.

Indoors, children played more quietly. A popular game, still enjoyed today, was cat's cradle, played with sinew string. Another game was played by tossing roots across the room, trying to make them land by touching a stake that had been driven into the earthen floor.

Northwestern children liked to collect and trade especially nice seashells or stones they found. There were abalone shells, mussel and clam shells, and most prized of all, dentalium. These tubular-shaped shells were highly valued for making earrings and necklaces. Often, adults working on special items would ask a child for a particular shell. The child was allowed to decide whether to trade it or keep it.

Coming of Age

Among northwestern coastal tribes, young people who had reached age thirteen or fourteen took part in special ceremo-

At a reservation in Glacier National Park, a Flathead mother presents her daughter with a new doll and other toys at Christmastime. Some Native Americans blended European holidays and spiritual customs with their own traditions.

nies. At one kind of ceremony, older women of the tribe danced around the girls and sang traditional songs, while tribal elders or the chief recited important tribal stories.

Often, a Tlingit girl who had reached puberty spent time alone in a small hut made of branches. Only close female relatives could visit her to bring food.

When the period of seclusion was over, wealthier families gave a feast, during which the honored girl wore new clothing. Yurok girls remained at home during a ten-day period but had to fast at least four days and sit with their backs to the fire pit.

Just before marriage, which might take place at age fifteen, girls of the Pacific coastal tribes were given tattoos on their chins as a sign of beauty and the fact that they were now married. Different designs were used.

Some coming-of-age celebrations included a *potlatch.* In the Chinook language, this word means "giving." It was a special feast, given at happy times, such as weddings, or in old age, when a person thought death was near. The hosts of the potlatch distributed fine gifts, such as blankets, cedar chests, otter furs, carvings, adornments, clothing, and even canoes.

It was a sign of great prestige for a person to give away his wealth or possessions. Sometimes people gave presents meant to make people laugh, since it was common to play jokes at potlatches. For example, a ragged blanket might be brought forth with great fanfare.

At the potlatch feasts, people ate deer, bear, seal meat, salmon, and whale bits, as well as sweets in the form of blueberries and currants. Bite-size pieces of food were arranged in wooden containers carved in animal shapes. People took their portions from these serving dishes rather than eating from individual plates.

"CHILD OF THE TOWN"

Among very wealthy men in the Northwest, it was the custom to give a potlatch—special feast—to pass on their noble titles to their children. These feasts included rituals and ceremonies that marked the child as being of high birth and to bestow the privileges and property that went with the family's rank.

Potlatches were traditionally held in the wintertime, since people had more stored food during these months to use at a feast. These were also gloomy, rainy days, a time when people especially enjoyed parties.

The oldest child in the family was chiefly honored at this potlatch, but younger children of the same parents were included, too. Young people were dressed ornately and perhaps tattooed. There were several days of feasting, then a holy man or guest chief pierced the children's ears or tattooed the girls' hands.

After the ceremony, the young person was entitled to be called noble—a *nyadi,* or "child of the town." As in all potlatches, the host followed the custom of giving gifts to all the guests. Those guests who had decorated the young people with tattooing, ear piercing, or other ornamentation would receive the finest gifts. A slave who had dressed the children honored at the potlatch was given his or her freedom. People of the highest rank gave eight potlatches for their children, who then had eight ear-piercings, four in each ear, to show their status.

At the final potlatch, held when they believed they were near the end of their lives, coastal Indians gave away their remaining possessions. As their ancestors had done before them, they followed the custom of giving away all earthly goods, preparing for the world beyond. Possessions were passed on to the younger generations who would, in turn, give their own potlatches as the cycle of births, coming-of-age ceremonies, and weddings continued.

Conclusion

By the mid-1800s, most Native American tribes had been displaced, their lands taken over by whites. They were confined to smaller parts of their old lands called reservations, often in unfavorable, unfertile locations. Some, like the Cherokee and Creek, were removed to Indian Territory in present-day Oklahoma. On these reservations, Native Americans tried to survive and adjust to sweeping changes in their ways of life.

In 1865, the U.S. government passed a law requiring that Indian children be sent to government-run boarding schools. This reflected a policy called assimilation—the idea that white ways were superior and that Native Americans should give up their customs and religions and try to blend into white society.

For decades, Indian children at the schools were forced to adopt the hairstyles and clothing of white people and use English instead of their native languages. They were taught Christian beliefs and religious practices.

Many Indians tried to avoid these schools, and the government stepped up its efforts in the late 1880s. Sometimes, U.S. soldiers physically took children against their will. This happened in the Hopi village of Oraibi in 1891 when 104 children were taken away. Blackmail was also used to coerce children into attending. When Chief Joseph, the famous

Nez Perce leader, refused to let his children attend the Fort Spokane Boarding School, the government said it would withhold food rations from the tribe, which was then living on the Colville Reservation in Washington State.

After leaving white schools, Native Americans often felt caught between two worlds. They had been torn from their own communities and ways of life but were not always accepted in white society or afforded equal opportunities for jobs, housing, health care, higher education, or other things. Where should they go? How should they live?

Misguided assimilation policies caused heartache and many problems. These policies were gradually abandoned during the 1900s as more and more white Americans realized how griev-

A group of Omaha boys at the Carlisle Indian School in Pennsylvania pose in their cadet uniforms. During the late 1800s, many Native American children were forcibly sent to white boarding schools.

ously Indians had been treated. During the 1950s and 1960s, the civil rights movement expanded as women and ethnic minorities protested that they were often treated unjustly. People showed increasing interest in their roots and heritage. Some Indian tribes went to court to gain economic compensation for the broken treaties that had robbed them of their lands and their traditional ways of life. They sought the religious freedom other Americans took for granted.

As the twenty-first century approaches, this pride continues to grow as Native Americans find ways to blend old ways with new. In 1984, Ross Swimmer, then serving as Principal Chief of the Cherokee Nation, said of the young people in his tribe,

> Many children are taught the ways of their ancestors, the Stomp Dance, and the religious significance of certain family traditions. Some also are taught about herbs and plant life and the medicinal value of those things. Many Cherokee children are growing up in families that are predominantly Cherokee-speaking, and the language is still very much alive.[1]

Nez Perce leader Cliff Smith voiced these sentiments in 1977, saying, "For years we have been taught that the only way to succeed is to be white. We must reverse that kind of education and teach Indians to be Indians. Along with skills we must teach customs, traditions, languages, and treaties."[2]

Commenting on how different life is for children today, a Sioux mother told author Richard Erdoes, "In the old days you had to be brave, even the children. You had to watch out all the time—for grizzly bears, Crow [an enemy tribe], and the U.S. Cavalry. But today, to grow up now, that takes real courage. With all the problems we have, every Indian child today has to be as brave as Crazy Horse or Sitting Bull."[3]

These days, Native American children grow up both on and off reservations. They face the problems of young people everywhere and others that confront their people. They study, work, and take part in sports and other activities. They enjoy watching television and listening to the latest popular music. They may grow up to be teachers, doctors, nurses, political leaders, fishermen, builders, lawyers, writers, artists, secretaries, scientists, farmers, performers, athletes, members of the armed forces—anything that any other young American might aspire to become.

Young Native Americans can be seen at summer powwows, kachina or harvest festivals, and other traditional gatherings. Here, they take part in the old songs and dances and hear the ancient words that link one generation to another in a circle that has no end.

Source Notes

INTRODUCTION

1. *Black Elk Speaks* as told to John C. Neihardt (Flaming Rainbow). (Lincoln: University of Nebraska Press, 1932), p. 1.
2. George A. Eastman (Ohiyesa), *Indian Boyhood* (New York: Dover, 1971), p. 3.
3. *Black Elk Speaks,* p. 7.

CHAPTER ONE

1. Lois Lenski, *Indian Captive: The Story of Mary Jemison* (Philadelphia: Lippincott, 1941), p. 105.
2. Lenski, p. 213.

CHAPTER TWO

1. John Ehle, *Trail of Tears: The Rise and Fall of the Cherokee Nation* (New York: Doubleday, 1988), p. 10.
2. James Adair, *Adair's History of the American Indian* (Johnson City, Tenn., 1930), p. 430.
3. William Bartram, *The Travels of William Bartram* (New York: Mark Van Doren, 1928), pp. 164–170.
4. Quoted in J. Ralph Randolph, *British Travelers Among the Southern Indians, 1660–1763* (Norman: University of Oklahoma Press, 1973), p. 150.
5. Bartram, p. 194.
6. Randolph, p. 76.

CHAPTER THREE

1. Quoted in Richard Erdoes, *The Rain Dance People* (New York: Knopf, 1976), p. 188.
2. Ibid. p. 184.
3. Quoted in Erdoes, *The Rain Dance People,* p. 187.

CHAPTER FOUR

1. Eastman, p. 15.
2. Quoted in Richard Erdoes, *The Sun Dance People* (New York: Knopf, 1972), p. 32.
3. Eastman, p. 44.
4. Ibid.
5. Eastman, p. 62.
6. Henry C. Roman Nose, "An Indian Boy's Camp Life," *School News,* (Carlisle Barracks, Pennsylvania), Vol. I, No. 1, June 1880, p. 1.
7. *Black Elk Speaks,* p. 53.
8. Ibid.
9. Quoted in *Black Elk Speaks,* p. 57.

CONCLUSION

1. Quoted in "Interview With a Chief," *Cobblestone,* February 1984, p. 40.
2. William Albert Allard, "Chief Joseph," *National Geographic,* March 1977, p. 432.
3. Erdoes, *The Sun Dance People,* p. 68.

Further Reading

Andrews, Elaine. *Indians of the Plains.* New York: Facts On File, 1991.

Burt, Jesse and Robert B. Ferguson. *Indians of the Southeast: Then and Now.* Nashville, Tenn.: Abingdon, 1973.

Calloway, Colin G. *Indians of the Northeast.* New York: Facts On File, 1991.

Cohoe (Nohnicas). *A Cheyenne Sketchbook.* Norman: University of Oklahoma Press, 1964.

Cotterill, R. S. *The Southern Indians.* Norman: University of Oklahoma Press, 1954.

Drucker, Philip. *Indians of the Northwest Coast.* Garden City, N.Y.: Doubleday, 1955.

Engel, Lor. *Among the Plains Indians.* Minneapolis: Lerner, 1970.

Erdoes, Richard. *The Rain Dance People.* New York: Knopf, 1976.

———. *The Sun Dance People.* New York: Knopf, 1972.

Hyde, George. *Indians of the High Plains.* Norman: University of Oklahoma Press, 1959.

Kroeber, Theodora. *Ishi: The Last of His Tribe.* Berkeley, California: Parnassus Press, 1964.

Lenski, Lois. *Indian Captive: The Story of Mary Jemison.* Philadelphia: Lippincott, 1941.

Liptak, Karen. *Indians of the Southwest.* New York: Facts On File, 1991.

Mancini, Richard E. *Indians of the Southeast.* New York: Facts On File, 1992.

Nabokov, Peter, ed. *Native American Testimony: A Chronicle of Indian-White Relations From Prophecy to the Present: 1492–1992.* New York: Penguin Books, 1991.

Sherrow, Victoria. *Indians of the Plateau and Great Basin.* New York: Facts On File, 1992.

White, Jon Manchip. *Everyday Life of the North American Indian.* New York: Holmes and Meier, 1979.

Bibliography

Armstrong, Virginia Irving. *I Have Spoken.* Chicago: Sage Books, 1971.

Bartlett, John Russell. *Personal Narratives of Explorations and Incidents in Texas, New Mexico . . . 1853.* New York: Appleton, Century and Co., 1854.

Beauchamp, William M. *The History of the New York Iroquois.* New York: Scribner's, 1913.

Binns, Archie. *Northwest Gateway: The Story of the Port of Seattle.* New York: Doubleday, 1941.

Catlin, George. *North American Indians: Being Letters and Notes on Their Manners, Customs, and Conditions, Written During Eight Years' Travel Amongst the Wildest Tribes of Indians in North America, 1832–1839.* Edinburgh: John Grant, 1926.

Eastman, Charles A. *Old Indian Days.* New York: The McClure Co., 1907.

Goddard, Pliny Earle. *Indians of the Southwest.* New York: American Museum of Natural History, 1931.

Hamilton, Charles, ed. *Cry of the Thunderbird: The American Indian's Own Story.* New York: Macmillan, 1951.

Irwing, John Treat. *Indian Sketches.* John Francis McDermott, ed. Norman: University of Oklahoma Press, 1955.

Jackson, Donald, ed. *Black Hawk: An Autobiography.* Urbana: University of Illinois Press, 1955.

James, George Wharton. *The Indians of the Painted Desert Region.* Boston: Little, Brown, 1903.

Josephy, Alvin. *The Indian Heritage of America.* New York: Knopf, 1968.

Lewis, Meriwether, and George Rogers Clark. *Original Diaries of Expedition.* R. G. Thwaites, ed. Boston: Houghton, Mifflin, 1953.

Morgan, Lewis Henry. *League of the Iroquois.* New York: Citadel Press, 1962.

Neihardt, John G. *Black Elk Speaks.* New York: William Morrow, 1932.

Ortiz, Alfonso. *The World of the Tewa Indians.* Chicago: University of Chicago Press, 1969.

Quaife, Milo M. *Chicago and the Old Northwest, 1673–1835.* Chicago: University of Chicago Press, 1913.

Randolph, J. Ralph. *British Travelers Among the Southern Indians, 1660–1763.* Norman: University of Oklahoma Press, 1973.

Red Fox, Chief William. *The Memoirs of Chief William Red Fox.* New York: McGraw Hill, 1971.

Talayeswa, Don. *Sun Chief: The Autobiography of a Hopi Indian.* New Haven, Conn.: Yale University Press, 1942.

Timberlake, Henry. *Lieutenant Henry Timberlake's Memoirs.* London: 1948.

Underhill, Ruth. *Workaday Life of the Pueblos.* Washington, D.C.: United States Indian Service, 1946.

Waters, Frank and Oswald White Bear Fredericks. *Book of the Hopi.* New York: Viking, 1963.

Wheeler, Homer W. *Buffalo Days.* Indianapolis: Bobbs-Merrill, 1905.

Index